T0130393

Alias Howard

....and so It Began for
an Adopted Child

R. FARMER

© 2023 R. Farmer. All rights reserved.

No part of this book may be reproduced, stored in a retrieval system, or transmitted
by any means without the written permission of the author.

AuthorHouse™
1663 Liberty Drive
Bloomington, IN 47403
www.authorhouse.com
Phone: 833-262-8899

Because of the dynamic nature of the Internet, any web addresses or links contained in this book may have changed
since publication and may no longer be valid. The views expressed in this work are solely those of the author and do
not necessarily reflect the views of the publisher, and the publisher hereby disclaims any responsibility for them.

Any people depicted in stock imagery provided by Getty Images are models,
and such images are being used for illustrative purposes only.
Certain stock imagery © Getty Images.

This book is printed on acid-free paper.

ISBN: 979-8-8230-0082-6 (sc)
ISBN: 979-8-8230-0083-3 (e)

Print information available on the last page.

Published by AuthorHouse 02/07/2023

authorHOUSE®

Alias Howard

Table of Contents

Chapter 1

I am an adopted child. That fact has followed me around like a summer shadow my entire life. I don't remember ever not knowing. Never-ending questions were as much a part of me as my fingers and toes. While the questions were always there in my mind, answers were scarce. In fact, they never came up in conversation. I remember being almost afraid to ask my questions, thinking it might be disrespectful or upsetting for the family, so I never did. The questions didn't go away; they just were not asked.

One year, my daughter was struggling with what to do for Father's Day, and she came up with the idea of researching my adoption, finding out what she could, wrapping it up in a nice neat package, and presenting it to me. This proved to be an impossible surprise, as I had to request some of the documents to help in the research. I signed the appropriate forms and returned them via email.

ol66

SOUTH CAROLINA **DEPARTMENT OF SOCIAL SERVICES**	**APPLICATION FOR POST LEGAL SERVICES** **ADOPTEE OR BIRTH PARENT**

I.   IDENTIFYING INFORMATION (ADOPTEE)

A.   Name: ___Robert_____Conner_____FARMER_____
            first   middle   (maiden)   last

B.   Address: ___2817 Park Ave._____Wilmington, N. C. 28403_____

      Home Phone: __(919)-762-0877_____ Work Phone: __(919)791-4802_____

C.   Date of Birth: __10-18-49_____

D.   Adoption Agency: __The Children's Bureau__ Date of Placement: _03-22-51_____

E.   Adoptive Parents: __Spy Wilbur Farmer, father, Anna Marie MArtin Farmer, mother_

      County of residence at time of placement: ____Richland_____

F.   Are you working with a Search Group? __No___ If yes, which one? _____

G.   Current address of adoptive parents: __Same as above, both deceased_____

II.   IDENTIFYING INFORMATION (BIRTH PARENT)

A.   Name: _____
            first   middle   (maiden)   last

B.   Address: _____

      Home Phone: _____ Work Phone: _____

C.   Child's Name: _____

      Sex: _____ Birth Date: _____

D.   Adoption Agency: _____ Date of Placement: _____

E.   Are you working with a Search Group? _____ If yes, which one? _____

III.   SERVICES REQUESTED

A. ☒ Non-identifying Information.

    ☐ I will be available for an office
    interview.

    ☒ I will be unable to come to your
    office for an interview. You may
    telephone me at the number given
    above.

B. ☒ Reunion Register (Counseling
    is available and is required by
    law before disclosure can be
    made. The Agency must contact
    the adoptive parents before
    the disclosure can be made.)

    ☐ I will be available for an office
    interview.

    ☒ I will be unable to come to
    your office for an interview. I
    prefer to receive a counseling
    brochure.

Once your name is on the register, you must notify the agency in writing if your address or phone number changes or if you wish your registration removed.

Signature: _Robert C. Farmer_   Date: _10/22/89_

Current Address of Adoptive Parents: _Spy W. FARMER 02/26/88_
Both Deceased _Anna Marie Martin Farmer 08/17/84_

DSS Form 3056 (Apr. 88) (Adopt)

2

Several months passed, over which the research began to fade from my memory, moving from the "anticipation" bin to the "oh well" bin. Then one day, as these things happen, the telephone rang, and the information was coming to me via email. In an instant, the details of my birth and my history arrived. It dawned on me at that moment this was the first time I, at age sixty-seven, had heard of how my actual birth went. What were the doctor's remarks and opinions? Baby Howard, six pounds ten ounces, was delivered by cesarean section. The baby was normal and healthy with dark blue eyes.

Further into the papers was my birth mother's account of the circumstances surrounding her pregnancy and her decision to place me for adoption. Information about her early life was included.

She was born to sharecroppers in rural South Carolina just before the Great Depression. She was poor and of modest living conditions, and was badly burned at eighteen months old by a boiling pot of lard her mother was cooking. At first, she was not expected to live. She spent the greater part of the next six years undergoing constant hospital treatment, several times for plastic surgery. This surgery greatly improved her appearance and allowed her to blink for the first time since the accident.

In all this information about her life, there were no names, no towns, no dates, just redacted spaces instead. The further I read, the more attention I paid to what detail was provided. I sought to figure out the county and community of her birth in 1918. A little girl getting terribly burned in a small community in rural South Carolina had to be newspaper worthy. And it was.

After some digging and googling, I decided to take a road trip. The community was only an hour or so down the road in Loris, South Carolina. One Wednesday morning, I struck out with notebook and pen in hand. I felt relatively confident I could find someone who would recall a little girl being so badly burned in 1920. They were described as churchgoing people. Surely an old timer at the church, *somebody*, could point me in the right direction.

███████ Howard

Born: October 18, 1949

Source: Letter received from Miss ███████████, Chief Division of
10-23-49   Child Welfare, State Department of PublicWelfare, Columbia,
             S. C., referring case of a mother in Sanders Memorial Hospital
             Florence, S.C., who wanted to place her infant son for adoption.
             The case had been referred to the Florence County DPW by Dr.
             ███████

10-25-49   See copy of case Work Director Smith's letter to Miss ████████
             accepting the case. CW Land who was in Florence would go by
             hospital and talk with mother.

10-25-49   CW talked with M in Saunder's Memorial Hospital on this date.
             M's baby was born 10-18-49.

M's story: M ███████████ was born ████████, 1918 in Horry County near
             ████████ /M was dreadfully burned when she was 18 months old.
             She pulled over a stand of hot lard which her mother had just
             made and the hot liquid had burned her face, head and parts of
             her body. She was rushed to a doctor who gave first aid and
             sent her on to the hospital. For some time the doctors felt that
             she could not live. M had spent the greater part of the next
             six years in ████████ Hospital in ████████ S. C. where she received
             constant treatment. Later she entered school. She made good grades
             and completed the 8th grade at the age of fifteen. At this time
             she quit school to help in the home, as her mother was in very
             poor health. M had been most fortunate not to have lost her
             sight. Her eye lids were dreadfully burned, but eyes were not
             injured.

             For several years M had received some plastic surgery at ████████
             Hospital. This had helped her appearance very much. She still
             needed more plastic surgery on her face. She was able for the
             first time since the accident to close her eyelids.

             M would have been a pretty girl if her face was not so scared
             and disfigured. She was badly burned on front of scalp and to
             the right side. She could partly cover this with her hair. M had
             very pretty brown hair. The doctor at ████ had tatooed eyebrows.
             This she felt helped her looks. M wore glasses, not from defective
             vision, but to shade her eyes, and hide the lids which were very
             much scarred.
                                                          to
             M had a very nice personality and seemed not/have any inferiority
             feelings about her handicap. M was also a very intelligent girl.
             She had made her plans as none of her relatives knew of her
             pregnancy.

             M was returning home from ████ Hospital early in January 1948
             and while waiting in Bus Station at ████████ N. C., a
             couple, man and wife spoke to her, and asked if she had been
             in an accident. M was wearing bandages on her face. They were
             very nice, kind and solicitous. After talking a while they
             told M that they were traveling toward ████████, and would be
             glad to give her a ride. She accepted this invitation and soon
             the three were riding on the highway. They were a young couple

My adoptive father, my *life* father, was a traveling salesman and had vast knowledge of people and their behavior. I remembered him telling me one summer as I traveled with him that to find out something in a small town, you go to the barbershop. I was off to the barbershop.

I scarcely even remember the drive. Thoughts raced through my mind. The questions never ended, one after another. I thought, *What if, what if I had grown up in this little town instead of my home?* My mind wandered to my friend from Iowa, who I had met some forty years before in Wilmington. I recalled how our children had spent so much time together. He had been there for me through the deaths of both of my life parents, and none of that would have happened if circumstances had been different. I was saddened at the thought of that.

I wondered what difference this short trip would make in my life. What would I uncover? I wondered if my mediocrity in my large city school would have been excellence in a small rural school. I wondered if I would have finally felt attached, part of the inner circle and not always on the fringes. The questions were endless. I was so engulfed in thought I almost missed the turn. That shocked me back to the reality of the moment.

A few more miles on the narrow road that led into Loris, past the funeral home and all the "First Churches" of all denominations with their neatly manicured lawns, the traffic became busier the closer I got to the crossroad town, It obviously had been divided by railroad tracks at some time in its past. Gone now, the tracks had been replaced by a center-of-town-type park/green space. The only remnant of the tracks was the bumpy intersection demanding a much slower speed to safely navigate them than was posted. After a left turn and a parking place on the west side of the tracks, I saw the barbershop staring me in the face.

Inside was a younger man with Marine Corps memorabilia displayed around him. The shop seemed to serve a couple of purposes other than one-chair barber services. As I looked closer, I realized it was a broadcast booth. I thought, *How amusing*, and *Boy, this is a one-horse town*. The man greeted me cordially and asked if I wanted a haircut. I told him a bit about the circumstance of my visit. Details of the narrative helped him reveal that some of my birth mother's relatives had been in the clothing business. I asked who the oldest clothier in the town was and quickly found out there was only one, and he was a third-generation owner.

My heart raced as I walked the half block crossing the abandoned railroad bed and entered the small-town store. I wondered if I was about to stumble upon a cousin. I did not, but what I uncovered was a man willing to help introduce me to folks around town—to the editor of the paper, to the town clerk, and to the radio show host. The radio show host told me about a talk show that aired from the barbershop on Friday morning. He asked me to come back and share my story on the air.

It was getting on toward midafternoon, and while I had found nothing concrete, doors had opened. Interest had been stirred, and I was coming back in two days to share my story in the hope that some of the over-ninety club, who were loyal listeners, might remember something of this little girl who was so dreadfully burned.

Chapter 2

The ride home was slightly disappointing and revealing—disappointing in that I had found no clues, no rabbit trails to follow; revealing in that I now understood the reality of the daunting task ahead of me. It wasn't going to be as easy as I had hoped.

Why were there no memories, no newspaper articles? I mean, in my hometown of Wilmington, North Carolina, I made the paper when I scored ten points in the YMCA Youth Basketball League. Certainly—hopefully—in such a small town, in two days the rumor mill would be working, and somebody would have an answer. Crossing the bridge, I had the thought that I might have to cross many bridges before this journey reached its destination.

I suddenly realized the ride to that part of the country had been made much faster by the new four-lane highway. The rhythm of the tires on every concrete seam took me back to the old two-lane road between Wilmington and my life grandmother. My brother and I used to play games in the back seat during those three-hour rides through rural South Carolina's tobacco belt. Friday afternoon trips on the old two-lane road were always much longer during tobacco season, taking us through every little town in between my home and my life grandmother's. Sometimes, the traffic would back up around the warehouses so badly we would stop and get a Coke and boiled peanuts and wait for dark to force the unlighted tobacco trailers off the road. Those Friday afternoon trips always ended with me sharing the bed with my grandmother or my aunt. Even as a kid, I didn't relish that idea very much. The next day, we would usually drive on to my other life grandfather's house over in upstate South Carolina, another four-hour drive up the road.

When my mind came to rest, I was in my driveway. The thoughts of the day began to give way to dinner and news and other events of the day. *I should sleep tonight after driving and talking all afternoon,* I told myself.

On Friday, I was up early in anticipation. The radio show was at ten in the morning. I pulled out of the driveway and headed back over the bridge. My thoughts again turned to the old two-lane road, and the many times I had traveled this very road with my family. It was the only way in and out of town headed west. Just after we crossed both bridges, we would bear right at the fork in the road and head to Florence, South Carolina, my life grandmother's home. The road paralleled the railroad tracks for about the first twenty-five miles, straight as an arrow. We called it the "dismal stretch"; it was so long and monotonous with nothing except pine trees, telephone poles, a railroad track, and the constant rhythm of the tires over the concrete slabs, which had spaces about every thirty feet. But I was bearing to the left today in search of the rest of the story.

That fork in the road was symbolic of a family that I knew and one that I didn't know. My entire life had been a right-hand turn at that fork in the road; this left-hand turn today was who else I would be. I no longer was the son of a flamboyant traveling salesman. I no longer had grown up in an upscale neighborhood. I no longer had a brother, and I no longer even had a name. This day, I was the son of a "dreadfully disfigured" woman, a lost child searching for family.

Without a format, an outline, or knowledge of this live platform, I became a bit anxious. Then suddenly, it was there. Inside the barbershop, I found a gathering of gospel singers and musicians, all the folks I had been introduced to on Wednesday, and a few more who were standoffishly curious, some wondering if they were going to find a cousin or brother hidden in the foliage of their family tree. Gospel Hour music, civic topics, local personalities, advertising, a break, and then it was my turn. Things moved along very quickly, and almost before it started, the program was over. And a brief narrative of the childhood circumstances of my mother—a mother for whom I didn't even have a name—was aired.

A reception of sorts followed in the shop. Everyone stood around and talked; some asked me questions—questions I didn't have answers for. That's why I was here. The town research librarian began to ask questions. I did have copies of the information to give to folks. She took one and exclaimed, "I am obsessive about things like this; I just have to know what happened." Little did I know what a pivotal part she would play in the events that were about to unfold.

The gathering dispersed. Folks headed home, to work, and to other activities that occupied their time in this very small town. I had done what I could do here. I had put the story out there.

All the way home, I thought about the research librarian. I couldn't help but believe that she would help me in getting the answers. What more could I do to help? I grew impatient during the hour-and-a-half drive. I quickly found that the information I had received did not satisfy my now-growing appetite for the whole story. I wanted to know names; I wanted to know as much as there was to know. I somehow felt I should already have the answers. It had been long enough (sixty-seven years), and I was on the doorstep, knocking on the door to the past. *Are any of the characters without names still alive? How would they treat me? What happened to the "dreadfully disfigured" woman who was my birth mother? Do I have brothers or sisters?* I knew my mother didn't want anyone to know about me then. What about now? My appetite took charge. *It doesn't matter what she wanted. I must know.* Determination had replaced idle inquisitions.

Several days passed as I formulated a plan to continue searching. I looked for old newspaper articles, rosters for employees at places mentioned in the information. I wished I were young enough to have "built-in" computer skills instead of having to seek out information without them.

I called the librarian, and called and called, until I was sure I had become a pain in the neck. There was silence on that end each time I called. Two days turned into two weeks of me staring at the fragmented information and very little else. Sure that I had exhausted the librarian's patience, I resisted the urge to call at least a dozen times. And one day, just as these things happen, my phone rang—the librarian. She greeted me, explained that she had been on vacation, and inquired as to my progress with the trips, the radio show, et cetera. I told her I had some interesting conversations, and the folks were great, but unfortunately, there was nothing concrete. Then the phone filled with "I have something." I don't remember much else about that conversation, just "I have something. I have a name."

I could scarcely believe what I was hearing; she was sending me all the names and family information via email, and I would have it shortly. I had barely disconnected the call when the email arrived. It had an attachment, which took a lifetime to download (forty-five seconds). There it was—family names, ages, birth dates, documented in the censuses from 1920 and 1930, which had just been put on the computers in South Carolina. Now what? I had the edges of the puzzle. All the corners were in place; the picture was beginning to reveal itself, each tidbit now filling in an empty space.

Sometime between 1920 and 1930, the family moved to the next county. When the 1920 census was taken, this family was the only family in this rural community to have only one daughter. They then reappeared in the neighboring county in the 1930 census with three additional children. Taking the ages of the siblings and other members of the household and comparing them to the nonidentifying information, I concluded that we had the right family.

United States Census, 1920 > United States Census, 1920 > South Carolina > Horry > Green Sea > ED 93

The door was open: Falba Ginnetha Lambert, born November 17, 1918, to Roland and Lila F. Lambert in Green Sea, South Carolina. My mother—she was ninety-eight years old, if she was still living. She had two brothers and two sisters, and they now lived in Mullins, South Carolina. My grandmother Lila was born in the next town west, Marion, South Carolina. These places were familiar to me. These towns were the tobacco towns I had traveled through in my youth on the way to see my life father's family. That was a strange coincidence; the left-hand turn in the road had twisted and turned and brought me back to the same towns and communities as the right turn. How very telling that would be in the next few days and weeks ahead as I fit the pieces of this puzzle together. What now?

I enlisted the help of a friend with whom I had been sharing the journey on that hour-and-a-half drive back from the barbershop, when I had felt impatient. Be careful what you wish for and even more careful what you pray for. Information came like a tsunami, completely swallowing me. There it was, the open door to the past and who else I was. I scoured the information and quickly found my grandmother's obituary, died in 1950.

...ila Frances Buffkin Lambert (1900 - 1950) - Find A Grave Memorial   http://www.findagrave.com/cgi-bin/fg.cgi?page=gr&GSln=lambert&G

Lila Frances *Buffkin* Lambert

Grandmother

Birth: May 11, 1900
            Horry County
            South Carolina, USA
Death: Dec. 30, 1950
            Mullins
            Marion County
            South Carolina, USA

Daughter of Elijah Leneau and Carrie Jones Buffkin, wife of Roland Lambert.

Family links:
 Parents:
  Elijah Leneau Buffkin (1876 - 1967)
  Carrie Jones Buffkin (1874 - 1930)

 Spouse:
  Roland Herman Lambert (1892 - 1966)*

 Children:
  Falba Ginnetha *Lambert* Montgomery (1918 - 1982)*
  Herman Martin Lambert (1920 - 1981)*
  Ravinell Lambert (1922 - 1928)*
  Howard D Lambert (1924 - 1994)*

 Siblings:
  Lila Frances *Buffkin* Lambert (1900 - 1950)
  Prudence Snow *Buffkin* Clemons (1907 - 1983)*
  B. C. Buffkin (1919 - 1932)*
  Edwin Leroy Buffkin (1932 - 2012)**

*Calculated relationship
**Half-sibling

Burial:
Mayers Memorial Park
Mullins
Marion County
South Carolina, USA

Created by: robin pellicci moore
Record added: Dec 30, 2011
Find A Grave Memorial# 82688281

MRS. ROLAND H. LAMBERT
MULLINS, Dec. 31, Special: Mrs. Leila Frances Lambert, 50 years old, resident of North Mullins died at her home Saturday night after two years of declining health.
  Funeral services, conducted by the Rev. Percy B. Upchurch and the Rev. Morgan Gilreath, will be held at 11 o'clock tomorrow morning from the Meares funeral home. Burial will follow in the Cedardale cemetery.
  Mrs. Lambert was the daughter of Elijah Buffkin and the late Mrs. Carrie Jones Buffkin. She was born in Horry county, but had made her home in Mullins for 37 years.
  Surviving besides her husband, Roland H. Lambert, is her father; two sons, Herman M. Lambert, of Mullins, and Howard D. Lambert, of Tacoma, Washington; three daughters, Misses Falba and Janet Lambert and Mrs. J. L. Jolly, all of Mullins; four brothers, E. L. Buffkin, Jr., Harry Buffkin, James Buffkin, and Edwin Buffkin; four sisters, Mrs. Ester Strickland, Mrs. Fred Curry, Mrs. Ross Clemmons and Mrs. George Poe.
  Added by: robin pellicci moore

Added by: Angie Ethridge McIntyre

Then my grandfather's, died in 1966.

Roland Herman Lambert (1892 - 1966) - Find A Grave Memorial   http://www.findagrave.com/cgi-bin/fg.cgi?page=gr&GSln=lambert&(

Roland Herman Lambert *(Grandfather)*

Birth:	Dec. 4, 1892
	Marion County
	South Carolina, USA
Death:	Apr. 3, 1966
	Mullins
	Marion County
	South Carolina, USA

Son of Elias Martin and Missouri Ann Bass Lambert. Married (1) Lila Buffkin, and (2) Mae Ernestine Harrelson.

Family links:
Parents:
  Elias Martin Lambert (1852 - 1929)
  Missouri Annie *Bass* Lambert (1857 - 1939)

Spouses:
—Lila Frances *Buffkin* Lambert (1900 - 1950)
  Mae Ernestine *Harrelson* Lambert (1898 - 1974)

Children:
  Falba Ginnetha *Lambert* Montgomery (1918 - 1982)*
  Herman Martin Lambert (1920 - 1981)*
  Ravinell Lambert (1922 - 1928)*
  Howard D Lambert (1924 - 1994)*

Siblings:
  Bessie *Lambert* Flowers (1881 - 1965)*
  Minnie *Lambert* Rogers (1883 - 1971)*
  Willis Elias Lambert (1886 - 1965)*
  Collin McCall Lambert (1889 - 1964)*
  Roland Herman Lambert (1892 - 1966)
  Lanneau Lambert (1898 - 1923)*

*Calculated relationship

Burial:
Mayers Memorial Park
Mullins
Marion County
South Carolina, USA

Created by: robin pellicci moore
Record added: Dec 30, 2011
Find A Grave Memorial# 82688287

R. H. Lambert

MULLINS — Roland Harmon Lambert, 73, died Sunday at his home.

Funeral services will be announced by Meares Funeral Service.

Mr. Lambert was born in Marion County, son of the late Elias M. Lambert and the late Mrs. Missouri Lamber, He was twice married, first to the late Lila Buffkin Lambert, then to Mrs. Mae Ernestine Harrelson Lambert.

Surviving are: his widow; two sons, Harmon Lambert of West Columbia and Howard D. Lambert of Tocoma, Wash.; three daughters, Mrs. Falba Montgomery of Columbia, Mrs. Aldara Jolly of Dentsville, Mrs. Janet Tanner of Sumter; a brother, John M. Lambert of Holly Hill; a sister, Mrs. Minnie Rogers of Mullins; 10 grandchildren and three great grandchildren.

Added by: robin pellicci moore

Added by: Angie Ethridge McIntyre

Both died in their home in Mullins, South Carolina. Every single time I made the right turn back at the fork in the road, it brought me through Mullins. In these obituaries, Falba Lambert is a surviving daughter in 1950, and then in 1966, she is Falba Montgomery of Columbia, South Carolina. She married! Then Falba Ginnetha Lambert Montgomery died February 10, 1982. I thought, *The end …*

I read further, and then something leaped off the page and really startled me. *"Surviving is a daughter"!* *I have a sister!*

Falba Ginnetha Lambert Montgomery (1918 - 1982) - Find A Grave ...   http://www.findagrave.com/cgi-bin/fg.cgi?page=gr&GSln=montgom

Falba Ginnetha *Lambert* Montgomery

Birth Mother

Birth: Nov. 17, 1918
Horry County
South Carolina, USA

Death: Feb. 10, 1982
Cayce
Lexington County
South Carolina, USA

Daughter of Roland Herman and Lila Buffkin Lambert, wife of Roy Montgomery.

Family links:
Parents:
Roland Herman Lambert (1892 - 1966)
Lila Frances *Buffkin* Lambert (1900 - 1950)

Spouse:
Roy Clyde Montgomery (1922 - 1974)

Siblings:
Falba Ginnetha *Lambert* Montgomery (1918 - 1982)
Herman Martin Lambert (1920 - 1981)*
Ravinell Lambert (1922 - 1928)*
Howard D Lambert (1924 - 1994)*

*Calculated relationship

Burial:
Celestial Memorial Gardens
West Columbia
Lexington County
South Carolina, USA

Created by: robin pellicci moore
Record added: Mar 21, 2014
Find A Grave Memorial# 126651336

MRS. FALVA L. MONTGOMERY

Mrs. Falva Ginnetha Lambert Montgomery, 63, of 1700 Harold St., Cayce, died Tuesday at Baptist Medical Center.

Born in Horry County, she was a daughter of the late Roland and Lila F. Buffkin Lambert. She was a nurse's aid at Baptist Medical Center.

Surviving are a daughter, Mrs. Irma Beck-Montgomery of Cayce; two sisters, Mrs. James L. Jolly of Camden and Mrs. Janet Tanner of Sumter; and a brother, Howard Lambert of Tacoma, Wash.

Services will be held at noon today at Dunbar Funeral Home, Gervais Street Chapel, conducted by the Rev. Barry Antley. Burial will be in Celestial Memorial Gardens.

Added by: robin pellicci moore

Cemetery Photo
Added by: Christopher

A second tsunami, this one much larger than the first: *No more obituaries, she is alive!* Information was coming faster than I could digest it. I got on the phone to my daughter, gave her a name, and *ping*. In thirty seconds, she had an address and phone number. I quickly dialed the number. No answer. And so it went for several days, then a week. My daughter found a picture on social media with Falba's name tagged. The picture was of a horse, in Georgia. As circumstances would have it, I have a friend in Georgia who is extensively involved with horses. Instant message time.

This friend had been following along with my journey, and quickly provided the name of the horseman who trained this horse. I called; the horseman was very protective of his client's privacy, so I quickly told him the story and asked if he would make a pre-call for me, telling the owner someone was trying to reach her in a matter of extreme importance. In the meantime, I wrote a letter and sent it by registered mail to the client's address. This way, I could track the letter, and the letter would require a signature, or else it would be returned in so many days.

The first attempt at delivery failed; notice was left at the residence. The days dragged by, and on the very last day that it could be picked up before it was returned, I received notification that it had been signed for. More silence—days, a week. Then on a Sunday afternoon, while I was on a quick trip to Walmart, wouldn't you know it, she called. She quickly grasped the opportunity to bow out that I offered by telling her I was in the store and I could call her right back. She was having dinner with friends and would be home around eight o'clock. We agreed I would call then.

The afternoon was filled with anticipation and a million questions I wanted answers to. I had to remember not to be aggressive. *Patience … breathe.* I felt younger already as I was reminded of how time had crawled by in anticipation of getting my driver's license. But I questioned myself: *Will she even talk to me? Does she believe the information? What if I am at a door that won't open? I must be grateful for this journey regardless of when it ends. I am grateful for the fragmented picture of the past even if it is just in black and white.* Baby Howard had a history. I had the big picture—one of those paint-by-number pictures from out of the past, untouched by the brush. I was ready for the color.

Eight o'clock arrived, and I dialed the number. My anxiety level rose as the rings continued (6, 7, 8, 9 … no answer). Now another set of anxious questions came to me: *What if her friends dissuaded her? What if I frightened her? I have always been told the tone of my voice is aggressive on the phone. Damn, can't*

I ever just tone it down? I tried calling four or five more times up till ten o'clock. I knew where she lived; I would go to her house if I had to. She would have to tell me to go away. I had come too far, learned too much, felt too much hope.

I thought I would have difficulty sleeping, but as quickly as I lay down and shut my eyes, it was morning. I woke with the same questions I had slept with and more. *What now?*

Days passed and turned into a week. My hope faded. Eager anticipation turned into fear of rejection. But I found myself strangely endowed with a tremendous amount of patience. She called once. Her interest was stirred; she was having some research done herself to validate or discredit what I had put to her. She would soon come to the same conclusion I had. She and I were viewing this from opposite sides. What I viewed as completing and giving closure to my life, well, would do anything but that to hers. It would be disruptive and upsetting. Obviously, she knew nothing of me, and it was 2016, so there were a gazillion scams out there. I expected this might turn out to be a closed door. I was just grateful I had found what I had found.

When I first set upon this path, I envisioned that it might lead to some revelation of who I was. I quickly realized that this journey began with two incredible women of great courage, women who were pioneers of many things. The journey was about two women who, while very different, were very much alike, so much so it was "goose bumpy" at times. I was bound at the hip and heart to both.

***

Both women were born in rural South Carolina, one upstate and one in Horry County. I spent a lifetime with one and never knew the other. One lost her mother in the influenza epidemic and had to become the mother to younger siblings, and the other had a very sick mother to whom she gave comfort and care from the age of twelve or thirteen. One of these women had a family with whom I was very close, and the other had a family I never knew. I could write a book with the knowledge I have of the first, but wouldn't you know it, this book ironically is more about the one I did not know and the impact her decision had initially and continues to have to this day.

This lady, my birth mother, was born in Horry County in 1918. Her father was a farmer and owner, which means the family was probably poor. When she was eighteen months old, she pulled a pot of hot lard from the stove and dreadfully burned her scalp, forehead, eyebrows, lips, ear, eyelids, and other portions of her body. She was treated by a local doctor for the emergency and taken to a hospital, where she was, for several weeks, not expected to live. She survived and underwent several surgeries at Duke. And at the age of six, she was finally able to blink for the first time since the accident. For three-fourths of her life, she was unable to blink. I try to imagine the loneliness she felt; it is beyond me.

By that time, the little girl had two brothers, and a sister on the way. She enrolled in school and, although initially behind, quickly caught up and was a very good student. She remained in school until the eighth grade, at which time she had to take care of her mother, who had a heart problem. This was in the early '30s. I wonder if the peer pressure of being disfigured and perhaps even being intellectually judged because of the dreadful disfigurement contributed to her having to take care of her mom.

Upstate, the other young woman, my life mother, was coming of age. In her class yearbook, one of her classmates remembers her as "pretty to walk with, witty to talk with." Her mother had died. All her siblings except for one were old enough to take care of themselves. This left her younger brother and her pharmacist father, who had been in a debilitating depression, in her care. He had lost his wife, his children were growing up, and he didn't have much motivation to move forward. The pharmaceuticals available today to treat depression were not yet available.

My life mother had an active social life. Her wedding several years later was the event of the season in the Greenville area. Her father's family members were prominent South Carolinians, holding public offices from judge to superintendent of education for South Carolina. They were educated, and she was probably a child of moderate privilege.

Years passed, and to my knowledge, these ladies' lives never intersected. Although they never knew of each other, these two ladies would have an anonymous relationship that left each eternally grateful for the other.

Little is known of the lady from Horry County before 1949, when she was again at Duke for another surgery to help with her disfigurement. Headed back to Horry County, she encountered a soldier—six feet tall or taller, with dark hair and a medium build—and his friendly wife at the bus station in what I believe was Fayetteville. They were solicitous, and for whatever reason, she accepted a ride with them as they were traveling to Columbia, where he was to be stationed, and would be traveling through what I believe was Loris or Mullins, South Carolina. Somewhere along the way, they stopped and had Coca-Colas and a snack, and shortly thereafter, she began to feel woozy. She woke up the next morning in a rest lodge room, naked and alone. Realizing she had been assaulted, she left the cottage and approached the manager, who was surprised to see her and asked where her brother was. She had been portrayed as a sister of the sergeant. The manager thought she had left before daylight with them.

She returned home, and to my knowledge never reported the incident or spoke of it to anyone. She did not realize she was pregnant until some months later, and never told her ill mother or father. Rather, she told them doctors had found an abdominal tumor during her last visit at Duke, and when the time came to remove it, she would have to return to Duke for several weeks for the surgery and recovery.

Things were going quite differently for my life mother upstate. She had fallen in love, married a flamboyant salesman from Florence, and moved to Charleston. They lived on the Battery at 23 Legare Street, and from there, they went to Columbia. After several years of trying, they had determined a physical problem made them incapable of conceiving as a couple. They adopted a baby boy while they lived in Columbia and then, in September 1949, transferred to Wilmington, North Carolina. They were unable to sell their home in Columbia immediately, so they found an inexpensive house on Wrightsville Beach (Harbor Island) to rent until the Columbia home sold. The salesman from Florence was traveling.

Raising their young adopted son in a new small community and trying to make friends must have been a lifestyle change for the attractive socialite from upstate South Carolina. The small beach community suited her. She made friends quickly, and she integrated into the tight-knit group of people who braved the winters in a relatively undeveloped area, in a home with no mechanical heat. In the middle of this, an event would change her and my life father's lives, and the life of the lady from Loris, South Carolina. One soldier, one woman, and a couple with an adopted child—who would believe that a confluence of events would bind these people together and change them all, and others, forever?

Mid-fall 1949, the woman from Loris was coming to term, and it was time for her to have the "tumor" removed. She left her mother and father completely unaware of her circumstance and checked herself into Saunders Hospital in Florence, South Carolina. With the assistance of a compassionate doctor, she brought a baby boy into this world on October 18. Two days later, she left the hospital and moved to another facility to complete her recovery from the C-section, a serious procedure in the late '40s. Twenty-two days later, the woman from Loris met with a caseworker, and the infant was placed with a temporary custodian and moved to Columbia, South Carolina. The caseworker's narrative states that the mother had difficulty dealing with the surrender but still reinforced her desire to place the baby for adoption.

Enter Baby Howard—weight six pounds ten ounces, with dark hair and dark blue eyes. The folks charged with foster placement met and decided that they would place Baby Howard with a couple who had already completed the screening process and indicated they desired a second child. Age was creeping up on the couple, the lady now thirty-five and the man forty-two. Soon, they would be outside the ages acceptable for adoption of infants. The couple had wanted a girl, but with the special circumstances as they were, they decided to accept the placement. The situation was this: the couple had left South Carolina and become ineligible to adopt for this reason. They, however, still owned their home in Columbia, and the authorities were unaware the couple had already moved to North Carolina.

The process moved along, and on December 15, the couple was informed they had been chosen and the procedure would go forward. Two days later, at the insistence of the woman, who now lived in Wrightsville Beach in a home with no mechanical heat, they were allowed to pick up Baby Howard so he could be with them for Christmas. She gathered a clothes basket, a pillow, and some cloth diapers and drove two hundred miles in the night, picked up Baby Howard, and brought him back to Wrightsville Beach without anyone knowing they had already left the state. On December 29, the couple, with both adopted children, headed to Columbia for the last visit with Baby Howard's supervising agency.

The narrative from that visit goes something like this: Baby Howard was gaining weight and had good coloring. The family had abruptly been called to move by the foster father's employer, and Baby Howard had been removed from the care of the doctor in Columbia and placed in the care of Dr. Sidbury in Wilmington, North Carolina. December 29, the caseworker suspended supervision. The excited couple returned to Wilmington, stopping in Effingham, South Carolina, to meet the paternal grandmother. The drive to Wilmington carried the family, with a new addition, through all the small tobacco towns along Highway 76—Marion, Mullins, Nichols, Fair Bluff, Chadbourn, Whiteville—and then that long straight road all the rest of the way until Leland, where it joined with Highway 17 at the fork in the road.

Somewhere along that highway that joined the red clay of Columbia and the sandy beaches of Wilmington, Baby Howard became Robert Conner Farmer (Bobby). That is what happened to Baby Howard.

STATE OF SOUTH CAROLINA,)
          :   CLERK'S CERTIFICATE
COUNTY OF RICHLAND.   )

     I, C. E. Hinnant, Clerk of the Court of Common Pleas and General Sessions for Richland County, in the State aforesaid, do hereby certify that the writing hereunto annexed consisting of two (2) pages, doth contain a full and true exemplification of the Decree issued in the Court aforesaid, in a certain case wherein "Spy Wilbur Farmer and Marie Martin Farmer" were petitioners and "The Minor known as Baby Howard, residing in the home of Spy Wilbur Farmer and Marie Martin Farmer, and The Children's Bureau of South Carolina" were respondents, as appears by the original records remaining in my office.

     IN TESTIMONY WHEREOF I have hereunto set my Hand and affixed my Seal of Office, at Columbia, South Carolina on the 22nd day of March, in the Year of our Lord, One Thousand, Nine Hundred and Fifty-one and in the One Hundred, Seventy-sixth Year of the Sovereignty and Independence of the United States of America.

              C. E. Hinnant
          Clerk of the Court of Common
          Pleas and General Sessions for
          Richland County, South Carolina.

What happened to Falba Ginnetha Lambert—the woman from Horry County, my birth mother—that Christmas season of 1949? Was she at home with her family? Did she tell anyone? I can only imagine the atmosphere. What was she feeling?

***

Why hasn't my sister called me back? I thought. *I'll write one last letter. No, I'll text. It will be faster.*

I know that all of this really has to be hard to wrap your head around. My adoption has not been a stone around my neck, and I certainly do not want to be a hindrance to you. While I wondered, more often than I realized, who, what, and why, I have never been consumed by a search. I was secure and safe and well cared for and afforded many privileges others were not afforded. My adoptive parents provided love and understanding and an upbringing in a home that valued the traditions of the South. We lived near the beach, so we were water lovers. I finished high school in 1968 (one year late because of an extremely social attitude). I went to college at Southeastern Community College in Whiteville, only about twenty-five miles from Mullins, SC.

My life grandmother lived in Florence, where my life father and grandfather were born and grew up. My grandfather was in the grocery business and my father followed and worked for Campbell Soup Co. He retired there in the early '70s. I entered the Navy in 1970 and was stationed in California and deployed to Vietnam on three different occasions. I lived in Upstate New York briefly after the military and worked for a standard breed horse trainer at Vernon Downs, NY, as a licensed assistant trainer. A relationship fell apart and I returned home to Wilmington in 1978, leaving a young son behind. Returning to Wilmington, I met a local girl slightly younger, fell in love. We have two children, a boy and girl, and I have a boy and girl outside of our marriage. So, four kids altogether; four grandkids, two boys (grown), two girls (eighteen and one); two great-grandchildren, both girls.

I have spent a lifetime living life. I have made mistake after mistake, but always get up and start over. Life has been good to me; I have experienced the world as few have. I have hitchhiked across this country and have participated in the recovery of a space capsule in the middle of the Pacific. I have climbed Yosemite Falls and hiked in Death Valley, I have sailed the seven seas and taken a flight in a fighter jet (two-seater). I have loved passionately and been brokenhearted. I have lived a full life. I no longer seek gain from situations, only to understand.

I have read this narrative of Falba Ginnetha Lambert Montgomery and find myself struck by her courage and her devotion to a sick mother for whom she sacrificed her youth to care for. Reflecting to 1949 is hard for me and I can only relate through my Southern upbringing. Mullins, SC, was a very thriving tobacco community back then, busy in spring and summer preparing for "cropping," and attitudes were very traditional. It would have been very difficult for a thirty-one-year-old "dreadfully disfigured" woman with a sick mother to care for her, never mind the addition of a newborn. I am a laid-back person, as I am told by my kids, and have lived with the blanks in my life for so long, I am certain that while I would love to know what her favorite foods were, what she liked to do, what kind of music she liked, was she funny or serious ... I would rather not if it will complicate your life.

I am sure of the authenticity of the information I sent you, and as a point of consideration, none of the information was researched by me. As I told the story in Horry County, people were captivated by the story of this little girl who had been so tragically burned and the other circumstances, they felt compelled to know what happened to this courageous little girl. I now can tell them what I know, only names. I remain hopeful that you will consider helping me fill in the blanks for those who have been touched by this five-foot-two woman whose life has impacted so many. This is not my story but hers.

Robert (Bob) Farmer

I hit the send button, and the continuation of this story was in her hands. It was Monday morning, the beginning of another week, and I wondered what, if any, response I would receive.

Later that very night, my phone rang, and I didn't recognize the number. Sometimes, I don't answer a number I don't recognize, but for some reason, this time, I did. It was her. She apologized for not calling back and explained the time that had passed since we first had spoken. My mind raced, and many of my questions didn't get asked. Her anticipation was evident, and I sensed she was having difficulty digesting the information. I asked if she had called because she got my text earlier, and she said no, that was not the reason; she could not receive text messages on the number she had given me, so she had not received my heartfelt plea. We talked about her reservations and how unbelievable all of this was for her—never a hint from her mother to her or her father about any of this, nothing from the family back in Mullins. I wondered how a woman could harbor such a secret for such a time, from 1949 to 1982, when she took it to her grave.

I almost missed what my sister was telling me while these thoughts flooded my mind, and then I heard her say, "We are not half brother and sister. I was adopted." The words fell on my ears like a clap of thunder from a bolt of lightning striking in the room. What! My thoughts went haywire. How could this be? I was more confused at that moment than ever before in my entire life. What the heck happened?

The story unfolded: my birth mother had married just a few short years after my birth, and after several years of trying, the couple decided to adopt. How much more bizarre can circumstances get? We both became drained trying to figure out what happened and where this was going to lead us. We had been thrown together by circumstances totally out of our control, and now here we were, unrelated and bound inextricably by them. I found her to be careful but engaging and willing to talk through this with me. I learned some about her life and she mine, and the conversation ended with a commitment to get back in touch.

Meanwhile, my wife and I were planning a trip to the mountains to celebrate a couple of coinciding events (Father's Day and our anniversary), and I wanted to meet my non-half sister, Irma, who was adopted by my mother after she gave me up for adoption. She lived only an hour or so away from the hideaway of a dear friend, who had been making it available to my wife and me for many years. I called Irma and agreed to meet in Lenoir, North Carolina, on Sunday. My wife and I drove to the mountains on the Thursday before Father's Day. The drive to the mountains was different this time. It had a purpose, not just an intimate getaway for a couple of old married folks. I wondered what the coming Sunday would unveil.

The trip was also different, but some things remained the same: chores. I had to trek down the hill to the back door at the cellar level. Opening the door, I smelled the mustiness filling the air; the darkness surrounded me as I stumbled to the panel box to flip all the marked breakers. Lights and no critters! I skipped up the stairs, sometimes two or three at the time, and unlocked the front door to a waiting wife with supplies in tow. I headed back to the car to retrieve the necessities she had packed for the three-day stay.

About an hour later, with everything inside, the air conditioner on and cooling, I sat down for a rest. Our weekend was filled with painting a few doors and relaxing on the south-facing deck. In the evenings, we would feed the deer and the raccoons. On one of our previous trips to the mountains, one of our friends developed a method of "coon fishing." He tied a piece of corn on the cob to the end of a piece of twine, tossed it off the deck, and waited for the coons to bite. It was hilarious, him with a beer in one hand and the twine in the other and the coon on the other end trying to solve the mystery of the corn that fought back. Saturday mornings, I would often hear the Tweetsie Railroad as it sounded the beginning of its workday with a few short bursts from the steam whistle.

Sunday, we touched base with Irma to find out she was en route. The trip down the mountain was different. I was not going to get groceries or sightsee or just take a country ride. I don't recall passing the hanging rock supported by a log or much of the ride on Elk Creek Road, which meanders along Elk Creek close enough in some places to see the trout swimming in the crystal-clear mountain water, and then rises to a switchback and some of the most scenic roadways in the state. The summer foliage clothes the naked branches of winter, the horses frolic in the fenced pastures, and usually, I would be consumed by these sights. Today, I was far too preoccupied. A very big moment was rushing upon me.

We arrived at the designated meeting place, and I decided to give Irma a call to see how far away she was. It just so happened she was at the stoplight across the street. She pulled up in her little car. I hopped out to open her door for her, and as I did, she exclaimed, "You look just like my Uncle Howard!" She had not a clue my mother had named me Howard at birth. She later told me that moment erased any doubt she had about the validity of my conclusion. Later in the day, as I showed pictures of my children, she identified them as "look-alikes" to my aunts and uncles she had grown up around.

Roland Lambert's Funeral
sons   daughter
Herman   Howard   Falba   3 grand
Lambert   Lambert   Montgomery   children

The questions I had for her were unending. Toward the end of the day, I could tell she was much more at ease. My wife stayed at the house while I took Irma back to her car. The hour-long trip to the car was filled with chatter, and after a while, Irma placed her hand gently on my arm and told me our mother had fostered nine children over the years. She related that she had prayed for a baby brother but that her mother would never foster a little boy, and now she understood why. Our brief visit ended with a real sense of connection for me, and I hoped Irma felt it too. I had many more questions.

The drive back to the mountain filled my mind with questions I never asked. Amid all the questions, there was a sense of quiet, a deep-down quiet, one that calmed the soul. The personal quiet allowed me to enjoy the ride through Buffalo Cove and its rustic farm and mountain buildings scattered along the hillsides, connected to the highway by steep driveways that were passable only by truck. I remember rolling down the window, smelling the freshness in the air, which seemed to enhance my sense of calm with its early-summer warmth flowing across my sleeveless arm as it rested in the open window. I enjoyed the ride along Elk Creek as much as any I had ever taken, recalling that I had just ridden it with a new friend, one who had quickly become dear to my heart. My mind wandered to the strange, even bizarre circumstances this friendship was founded on. I thought, *Why not?* Each turn in the road of this journey held a surprise. I kept pinching myself to reassure me of my consciousness and reality.

The drive back to Wilmington had been I-40 East. That day, we took a different but very familiar route on Highway 74, now known as the I-74 corridor. The highway had changed, and the only reminders of the small tobacco towns driven through in my youth were signs with their exit numbers and names in reflective white paint. The character of the people was no longer visible in the monotonous interstate landscape. Somehow, that "dismal stretch" had, in its modernization, gotten longer and lonelier, and I thought about how the modernization of life through technology had the exact opposite effect on my personal journey. The absence of technology had prevented the discovery of all of this until recently.

Summer arrived, and life at the beach was busy with visitors coming and going. While on a trip to Texas to see my daughter and her family, I had the opportunity to share the information with them and give a more complete synopsis of the meeting with Irma. On a trip later in the summer to Upstate New York, I was able to share with my son Ryan and granddaughter Caitlynn, who had just graduated from high school.

Phone calls and texts with Irma had become regular treats, and we had established a more trusting relationship. Irma's husband, Steve, worked out of town a lot, and I had not met him. We had scheduled several beach trips, but Labor Day arrived, signaling the close of summer, and none materialized. Irma had been working a long schedule because of a heavy demand for her. I held out hope and was gently persistent, and finally, she agreed to come in mid-October around my birthday.

The time between June and October found me searching for more answers. What were the circumstances surrounding Irma's adoption? Why was my mother unable to conceive again? How could my mother keep the facts of my being surrendered for adoption secret through the screening process?

The conversations with Irma in those months revealed some answers and the importance of my mother's secret. One of our early conversations centered on Irma's adoption and how unreal these circumstances were. During this conversation, I learned that Irma had been adopted in Europe! Pieces were falling into place again. They were stationed in Europe after the war and adopted her while there. My mother had avoided the screening process and preserved her secret.

I had heard about eugenics in the news before and had not paid much attention to it, but sometime during this period, I began to research South Carolina's history in eugenics. The information was startling. The law was passed in 1930 and continued until 1962. The law was written to apply to those with inherent mental and physical disabilities. Had my mother been a victim of this inhumane procedure? I wondered if the doctor had performed the procedure secretly, perhaps believing this woman who had obvious scars would never marry or want to have children again. Or was the procedure due to a complication of my C-section birth or even a judgment of her mental state based on the physical disfigurement? My research led me down the path of speculation, and as I had already learned, speculation often masks the truth. So I left this alone and decided that the issue was not important, at least not for the moment.

Mid-October sneaked up on me, and before I knew it, Irma was pulling into my driveway to celebrate my birthday. Try to imagine this if you can: I was sixty-seven years old, and this was the second time I had laid eyes on Irma, and I needed to ask her some questions. She almost answered my questions before I asked them. She wanted to ride to Mullins and Green Sea and Conway to meet Marianne Rhine, the research librarian. We went for a birthday dinner, returned home early, and turned in for the night. The following day would be full, four and a half hours of drive time, and who knew how long we would spend at each place looking and searching.

Wednesday morning, Irma was up, and we were on the road before 8 a.m. First stop: Mullins, South Carolina. This trip began with the crossing of that familiar bridge that led to the highway west or south, to that fork in the road. It was different this time … I knew. We took the new sterilized four-lane highway sixty miles west to Chadbourn, where we exited and got on the old scenic route. Hurricane Matthew had blown through with torrential rain in the region, leaving all those little towns flooded and blocked off except to residents. Everywhere we looked, centuries-old oaks were blown down; whole stands of pine trees bent to the prevailing wind; roofless buildings dotted the rural landscape. There were men clearing the trees, sheriffs and highway patrol pointing the way through the twisting detour routing us around Fair Bluff. The town had been inundated with the twenty-one-feet-above-flood-stage water levels along that stretch of the Lumber River. We eventually were back on that tobacco road I had traveled in my youth. In those days gone by, my life father would have traveled through Fair Bluff to Fairmont, then back to the highway by way of Main Street in Mullins. He liked to stop at a country store over that way and pick up boiled peanuts. It was a little out of the way, but he didn't care.

We passed through Nichols, and our talk shifted from small talk to the business at hand. Irma wanted to go to my birth grandparents' grave. From there, she felt she would find the old house. We stopped at the library to locate the cemeteries. There were four—two just down Main Street, and two a little farther out on the highway. A few blocks down Main Street, just past a dilapidated but still occupied motel littered with bicycles, cooking grills, table umbrellas, an inflatable kiddy swimming pool, and a couple of broken-down cars, was the entrance to the first cemetery. Two groundskeepers were busily working, cleaning up limbs and leaves and branches from the storm just two weeks prior. I unhopefully made an inquiry about the location of graves. Surprisingly enough, these men were "the authority" on this cemetery, and the one directly across the street, as it turned out, was our destination.

Directed to a part of the cemetery that was filled with my birth family's last name, we began to walk around, looking for Roland and Lila Lambert. I found myself humming the tune from the point in *The Good, the Bad and the Ugly* when three hombres are searching a cemetery for buried gold—a Henry Mancini tune. I was searching for gold of a different kind, family roots and connection.

Then I almost tripped over it, the headstone—Lila Francis on the left and Roland Herman on the right. The stone was darkened with age and the black mildew that obscured the dates and the inscriptions. I was surrounded with the small granite markers of my ancestors, all of whom I never knew. My chest heaved. The whole inside of me swelled. The old saying, "A rabbit ran across my grave," used to depict a shiver-inducing situation fails to describe the emotional rush I had. I called out to Irma. She turned and in a few short steps was reminiscing about family members almost as if I had been there with her way back when and remembered the characters just as she did. I was emotionally confused. I felt like the new kid on the block, nodding in agreement and acknowledgment and not having a clue who or what she was talking about. She had all the family knowledge and was not. I had none … and was. I was jealous and grateful, resentful and compassionate, swinging from one emotion to the other, an emotional grandfather clock.

Sometime later, we made our way back out to Main Street, turned right, and headed farther out of town in search of the old family home. Irma's faded memory was all we had to go on. We found a house that she believed to be the place. We inquired of the next-door neighbor about a quarter of a mile down the road and were directed to the owner just down the road. He was not at home, so we left a note with both our numbers.

We turned south and set a course for Conway and the meeting with the librarian who had been so instrumental in discovering my origins. We had about an hour drive through the rural farm country that my birth mother had grown up in. I wondered if she had ridden these same highways and even seen some of the same sights. More devastation from the storm was everywhere, power crews with their boom trucks and caution cones occupying half of one lane. Drivers on the road were rubbernecking to see it all and slowing traffic to a crawl. The slow traffic gave me time to catch Irma up on my relationship with the librarian and let her know Marianne had spent a lot of time connecting the dots. I had waited for the librarian to give the details of her conclusion based on the information she had. I had watched it unfold, and her forensic mind still amazed me.

Finally, off the country roads, we moved on to the busy four-lane highway that connected the Upper Piedmont region of South Carolina with the coastal beaches and the high-rise beachfront condos, replacements for the once-unheated beachfront weekend homes that lined the wide, white sandy beaches from Myrtle Beach to Pawleys Island. Conway snuck up on me. The library was just off the highway and easily accessible. We walked through the entrance and asked for Marianne. She was expecting us.

I heard the receptionist call the newspaper section and announce our arrival. Marianne appeared from the stacks with an armful of files and papers and no other stereotypical characteristics. Energetic, engaging, and not exactly quiet, she began to lay out the papers and describe the process she used to uncover the redacted information I had received only six months prior.

She first searched for newspaper articles about a burned baby girl (my birth mother) from 1918 forward. Finding no results, she turned to the census from 1920. She had determined the last name ended in the letter *t*. The last letter had been left partially readable because manual redaction with a black marker had fallen just short. She compiled a list of last names that ended in *t*, searched the 1920 census of Horry County, and found only one family with a little girl under two years old. The family disappeared from Horry County records for the 1930 census and reappeared in the neighboring county with the addition of siblings who matched the ages and descriptions provided by the South Carolina adoption folks in the nonidentifying information I received last December.

A newspaper reporter/human interest writer of the *Horry Independent* scurried through the front door of the library with notebook and camera in hand and introduced himself to Irma. We had met several months earlier at the barbershop in Loris. He kinda reminded me of Jimmy Olsen, boy reporter in the Superman television series. Dozens of questions and several photographs later, he related to us the unique nature of this story. He expressed his hope that his publisher would allow him enough time to complete the story properly.

Conway librarian brings siblings together

BY ROBERT ANDERSON
ROBERT.ANDERSON
@MYHORRYNEWS.COM

Finding lost siblings is nowhere in the job description of Horry County Memorial library assistant Marianne Rhine.

But that was the result of some of her recent research as she helped a 67-year-old North Carolina man locate a sister that he didn't even know existed.

Bob Farmer of Wilm-

> *"I've often wondered if I had any siblings and I don't have to speculate anymore. We're just going to let it happen as it happens. We're going to let the relationship develop. We're both without parents now and not much family."*
>
> **Bob Farmer**
> brother

ington, N.C., contacted the library in March hoping to find the mother who gave him up for adoption shortly after his birth. He contacted the Horry County Library because he knew that his mother was born in Loris.

"He called in March and asked me if I could find an article on microfilm about his mother," Rhine said. The only information that Farmer provided was his mother's birthday and the news that she was severely burned and badly disfigured in an accident involving hot lard when she was only 18-months-old.

When Rhine was un-

able to find a story about the accident she asked Farmer if he could provide additional information.

Farmer was able to produce a packet of information that his daughter obtained from the S.C. Adoption Reunion Registry while researching her father's family hoping that it would be a special birthday gift.

Included was a brief history of Farmer's mother's family including the names of her siblings, aunts and uncles.

Rhine quickly tracked down Farmer's mother's obituary, and he was surprised to learn that he had a younger sister named Irma, who happened to be living about 300 miles from Wilmington in Columbus, N.C.

Farmer contacted his sister, who wasn't immediately sure that she wanted to talk with him let alone meet him. She didn't respond to his letters and telephone calls for about a month.

"I was like what is this?" she asked. "Who is this person? I think I read it five times. I was apprehensive. I was very shaken. I was very slow in this whole process. I just couldn't accept it. I was frozen with apprehension."

Although Beck-Montgomery knew about her mother's accident and the fact that her face was disfigured in the accident, she didn't know the entire story.

"It's a tragic, tragic story," Farmer said. "While she was traveling back and forth from Mullins to Fayetteville for facial reconstruction surgery she encountered a couple who offered her a ride. They drugged her and she woke up the next

morning and realized that she had been assaulted. The doctor colluded with her and said that she had a tumor that had to

be removed. When the time came, she went to a hospital in Florence where I was born."

According to Farmer, his mother apparently decided to place him up for adoption because she was 31-years-old and living with her family in Mullins at the time of his birth. He believes that his mother was also caring for her own mother, who died just two months after he was born.

Farmer was adopted by a couple from North Carolina, who previously lived in Columbia and still had a home in South Carolina. The couple had

previously adopted another son.

"They had already moved to Wilmington when they adopted me," Farmer said. "If they hadn't had a house in South Carolina they couldn't have adopted me. My mother and father provided for me. I went to the best school and lived in the best neighborhoods."

Despite her reservations, Beck-Montgomery finally returned Farmer's call, and agreed to meet him for the first time on Father's Day in Lenoir, N.C.

"I didn't tell anyone where I was going and why," she said. "I was like what am I doing? I even texted a friend and said I'm in a CVS parking lot in Lenoir in case I don't ever come back."

The initial meeting was cordial and lasted only a few hours.

"The first time we met she got out of the car and

said 'you look like Uncle Howard,' " Farmer said. "Mom and Howard were very close. I still have a hard time thinking about a brother."

The two text and talk to each other often, and met for the second time this past week when Beck-Montgomery drove to Wilmington to spend a few days with her brother, including his 67th birthday. They drove to Conway to thank Rhine for the role she played in their reunion.

"We would have never met had it not been for her," Farmer said. "I've often wondered if I had any siblings and I don't have to speculate anymore. We're just going to let it happen as it happens. We're going to let the relationship develop. We're both without parents now and not much family."

Beck-Montgomery doesn't have any children, but Farmer has two children, two grandchildren and two great-grandchildren.

Beck-Montgomery doesn't want to rush into things, but is interested in maintaining a relationship with her newfound brother.

"I'd just like to develop a close relationship," she said. "This trip has been very educational. I've seen pictures. I'm an aunt. Even if we don't have a loving relationship we can have a friendship, it's a work in progress. We're trying to take it day by day and develop a relationship. I don't want to force anything."

Beck-Montgomery still finds it hard at times to believe she has a brother.

"It's like one of those dramas you hear on television," she said. "No one would believe it. I just like the idea of having a baby brother."

According to Beck-

Montgomery, her mother never told her she had an older brother.

"Mom never said anything about this whole incident," she said. "She kept it under cover. She moved to Columbia after he was born, and met my dad at Fort Jackson in 1952. She was 63-years-old when she died in 1982."

Although she hasn't been around her brother very much, Beck-Montgomery said she can see a connection the two share.

"I think it's more his approach to life and people," she said. "She was very knowledgeable and he's the same way. He likes people and wants to be around people. I think just his approach to life is reflected in the way mom approached life."

Farmer believes that God played a part in bringing the two together. He said his daughter prayed before starting to research his birth family shortly after his life parents died way back when the Internet was just getting started.

"What God originates, He orchestrates," Farmer said. "This has been extremely revealing and rewarding to me. I've learned a whole lot about myself. It's been a good deal. It's a new beginning. It's a new chapter. It's a whole new book."

Rhine is happy to have played a role in helping the two connect.

"I'm ecstatic that they have found each other and he can learn about his family," she said.

WHAT IS PRIVATE MORTGAGE INSURANCE?

By: Katie L. Brookshire

If a buyer puts down less than 20 percent of the selling price on the mortgage, lenders may require the buyer to buy another type of insurance called private mortgage insurance (PMI). This provides insurance to the lender in case the buyer is not able to repay the loan and the lender is not able to recover

AAST students inducted into the

City of CONWAY SOUTH CAROLINA

The ride back on the new and improved four-lane highway was much faster. My mind wandered to Irma's responses to some of the questions from the reporter. She described herself as "frozen with apprehension" and "wanting to develop a close relationship." She liked the "idea of having a brother." I thought to myself we had arrived at the place and time for me to share some of the threads that had woven their way in and out of each of our lives and created this patchwork we would call *family*. We bypassed the little towns, and while Irma recounted the day, I began to organize my thoughts.

Some time passed while I tried to get all the threads assembled into a fabric that would show Irma how close we had been all these years. Each "coincidence" was a thread of a different color.

> The circumstances that helped me locate you are these: A friend of fifty years happened to be involved in horses down in the South Carolina/Georgia area and recognized the trainer of your horse Superman from a newspaper picture where you were named. A classmate from high school, who coincidentally was skilled at searching after doing ancestry research on her own family, quickly tracked you down through Findagrave. com, where you were listed as a survivor in our mother's obituary. My daughter, who is working in an office where they use some tracking and reporting tools, soon had your name, address, and phone number. All these circumstances and many more brought us together.
>
> Marianne Rhine, the librarian who was so touched by the story of our mother, became obsessed with the search and used that very word: *obsessed*. There are the folks in Loris who so selflessly took their time to humor me and encourage me in the search.
>
> Then there is Roy, Falba's husband. He was from a small town in the Midwest, Stanwood, Iowa. By coincidence, the friend I met forty years ago is from Stanwood, Iowa. His father and Roy Montgomery were the same age. I would think little of such a "happenchance," except that the real possibility that he met our mother exists. My friend has a brother your age who attended the same university as you in Iowa. While this had little to do with our connecting, what are the chances?

My life cousins in Columbia, South Carolina, where you grew up, are all your contemporaries—hard to imagine you never crossed paths. I visited my life uncle, who was a longtime patient at the Baptist Hospital in Columbia, where our mother worked for many years.

The many threads that are colored in irony, the geographical connections to my life parents and birth parents, are remarkable. I passed through Mullins and Columbia each time I visited my life grandparents, sometimes directly by my birth grandparents' home and later their grave sites, without a clue until now. The visits to my life grandfather in Greenville, South Carolina, carried us through Columbia, within miles most times, and on one occasion within blocks, of your homeplace.

Both of my mothers sacrificed much of their youths to care for all or part of their families at some time. They both lived in dysfunctional families that required far too much of them with little in return, yet each of them chose to continue to care for others until their deaths. I always admired my life parents for their sacrifice, and I now find myself in the enviable position of knowing that the first two ladies in my life were selfless and loved children. My life mother demonstrated that when adopting me, and my birth mother demonstrated it by surrendering me and then fostering nine children (all girls) and adopting you.

My life brother, Billy, was severely burned as a preteen while delivering newspapers. He had skin graft surgeries, and my life parents' time and resources were consumed by this event. I recall now, with some degree of guilt, the envy I had at the time.

That brings us to the irony of all ironies, you and me. We are both adopted, and while we share no DNA, we share your life mother and my birth mother. I immediately assumed a DNA connection when I read our mother's obituary and ironically find myself in a sibling relationship with someone I have more in common with than if we were linked by DNA.

A military man from Virginia, tall with dark blue eyes, and his wife with him—the only mention of my father in my mother's narrative. That's not much to go on. Where do I begin to search for the rest of the story? Do I have other siblings? Is my father alive? Where do I begin? I have no hints; I have no narrative.

Some time has passed, and the passion of the search has been somewhat satisfied by the developing relationship with Irma, but the questions linger. A trip to Texas to visit my daughter and her family found me in a conversation about all these things, and as usual, her intuition about my curiosity was correct. I must know, but how?

Several weeks later, a package arrived at the front door. It was from Ancestry.com, a DNA swab test compliments of my daughter. This was too easy: swab my cheek, and send it in. With that done, waiting the anticipated six weeks to three months began. No Marianne to call, no barbershop, no small-town "heroes" … this waiting was different. There was nothing to do but wait and wait and wait.

Then, one day when I checked my email, there they were—the results. I read the cover letter about closest relatives and other factors that played into the compiling of eight pages of relatives. And those were just the ones who had been tested. Names, relationships, email addresses—these were the folks eager to be contacted. Here was all the information laid out before me … everything except who my father was. What now?

The next day, as I checked my email, I saw contacts from people I didn't know. How would I sift through these to get on track to discovering my father's name?

I contacted Bob Lucas, a fellow I had known for some time who turned out to be a third cousin through a shared a maternal great-grandmother. Bob had vast knowledge of the maternal side of our family and had done the DNA swab. Maybe he could suggest a sorting method. He eliminated all the matches we had on the maternal side, leaving nothing but the paternal side, except for a few.

I began looking for the closest relatives—first cousins, uncles, or half siblings. I began the search only to be interrupted by an email from Michael Karabelas, already identified as a second or first cousin by Ancestry.com, identifying his father as Lewis Ashton Cassidy. I searched Findagrave.com and located his obituary. He died early, at age forty-one, with *no siblings*. How could Michael and I be cousins? His father had no siblings, and his mother was from Greece but living in Virginia with her parents when she met and married Lewis, who was in the Navy and stationed in Norfolk at the time. We were not first cousins! We were half brothers, and that was only part of it.

Some days later, another communication from Michael told me of a half sister, Beverly Gordon. Beverly lived in Matthews, North Carolina. Michael gave me contact information for Beverly. I contacted her, and we spoke on the phone several times over the next few months. Beverly was engaging and willing to help me fill in the blanks. We needed to meet.

A planned trip to visit my daughter in Texas would provide an opportunity on the return trip. We planned to meet for lunch in Matthews, where I found Beverly and her husband, Wes, engaging and not at all surprised that another half sibling had turned up. She described to me a man who was a bit of a scoundrel, an overbearing man, a chauvinist, someone who lived his life without fear of consequences, and definitely a "rambling man."

The many coincidences in our lives were about to present themselves, and they were astounding. Beverly grew up on Central Avenue in Charlotte and lived there during her mother's marriage, separation, and divorce from our father. Those had little to do with me except that Central Avenue was the old homeplace of my life grandmother, Eloise Sadler. Her marriage to my life grandfather, F. H. Martin, prompted her to move to Greenville, South Carolina, leaving her sister Birdie to live in the home, where I visited on more than one occasion. And as I discovered, Beverly was living on the 700 block of Central Avenue while I visited the 500 block. During this visit, I also discovered that Beverly's daughter purchased a home in Wilmington, North Carolina (my hometown), on property that a former neighbor of mine, Dr. Arnold Sobel, owned. There were two other half siblings on my father's side from his third and final marriage, both now deceased, as well as his wife. Lewis was the fire chief at the Hampton Roads shipyard where my sister-in-law and her husband worked.

The journey of discovery is over … at least for the moment. The doors have all been opened, the questions have been answered, and the peace of knowing has replaced the nagging question, "Why?"

Many say the people of the world are divided or separated by only six degrees; that must be an average. People in my life have proven to be so closely intertwined. I now understand why I have felt at home wherever I am. When I view my characteristics, I can see the influence of both my biological family and my life family. We are who we are regardless of name, and we are products of both genetics and our environment.

Printed in the United States
by Baker & Taylor Publisher Services